First published in Great Britain by HarperCollinsEntertainment 2006
HarperCollinsEntertainment is a division of HarperCollinsPublishers Ltd,
77 – 85 Fulham Palace Road, Hammersmith, London, W6 8JB

The HarperCollins children's website address is
www.harpercollinschildrensbooks.co.uk

The Official Mary-Kate and Ashley website address is
www.mary-kateandashley.com

1 3 5 7 9 10 8 6 4 2

ISBN-13: 978-0-00-722898-0
ISBN: 0-00-722898-8

Printed and bound in China

mary–kate andashley

beauty secrets

beauty hints, tips & advice for every day

www.mary-kateandashley.com

DUALSTAR
PUBLICATIONS

HarperCollins*Entertainment*
An imprint of HarperCollinsPublishers

mary–kateandashley
beauty secrets
beauty hints, tips & advice for every day

www.mary-kateandashley.com

DUALSTAR
PUBLICATIONS

HarperCollins*Entertainment*
An imprint of HarperCollinsPublishers

Hi!

Welcome to **mary–kate**andashley Beauty Secrets. Looking good on the outside isn't just about the make-up you wear or a cool hairstyle – it's about feeling great on the inside.

We've pulled together the best advice on how to play up your best features, how to hide some of the not so great ones and, most importantly, how to keep yourself healthy. There's a whole section on how to make the most of your make-up box and heaps of different looks for you to try.

Always remember – make-up should be fun. Rules are made to be broken so don't be afraid to try something new!

contents

1 beauty basics

Beauty Basics is exactly that, getting back to basics. You wouldn't expect a great artist to try and paint a masterpiece on some tatty old canvas, would you? So how can you expect to get the best make-up results if you're not working with great skin?

Honestly, very few people are born with perfect skin. It takes a lot of work, tonnes of water, plenty of exercise, and, in the case of most photos you see of models in magazines, hours of airbrushing to get your skin looking perfect.

Don't let the beauty mags fool you, the best things for young skin isn't really expensive creams and lotions – it's diet and exercise! Sorry girls, time to get your running shoes on!

get out what you put in

The first and most important thing you can learn about looking great is that you get out what you put in. If you sit around on the sofa all day, watching TV, eating junk food and drinking fizzy drinks, your skin and hair are going to look lifeless and dull.

Everyone needs to eat five portions of fruit and vegetables each day. That might sound a lot but it really isn't! Try blitzing a banana, five strawberries and an apple every morning – there, that's three of your daily portions in one tasty smoothie!

It's hard to work out how much one portion is so here's some handy guidelines:

One apple
One banana
Half a cup of tomato
Half a cup of sweetcorn
Five strawberries
Two pieces of broccoli
One carrot
Half a cup of peas
One small glass of fresh juice
Half a cup of lettuce

It's also important to drink plenty of water, about five tall glasses a day. If you don't drink enough, it will show in your skin, hair and nails, and you might even start to suffer headaches and dizziness! This is your body's way of telling you you're dehydrated.

what's your skin type?

* So now you're eating all the right things and drinking lots of water but your skin still doesn't look right. Could be that you're using the wrong products for your skin type.

* To find out what skin type you have, try this test. It's perfect for a sleepover!

* Wash and dry your face with a neutral cleanser and water. Pat it dry and leave it, no moisturiser, for a couple of hours (or the length of your sleepover movie!) Now press a single piece of tissue paper against your skin. How does it look?

* If no oil comes off on the paper and your skin feels soft and smooth, lucky you! You have normal skin.

* If oil comes off your t-zone (your nose, cheeks and chin) you have oily skin.

* If there's no oil but your skin feels dry and tight, then you have dry or sensitive skin.

* If your nose feels oily but your cheeks are dry and tight, you have combination skin and need to use two different regimes for the different areas of your face.

skincare for normal/oily skin

If your skin is normal to oily or combination, then this skin care regime is for you!

A wash off cleanser works best for oily skins. Wet your face, lather the cleanser in your hands and massage onto your face, avoiding the eye area, in a circular motion. Pay special attention to your oiliest areas. Now pat your skin dry. You don't need a toner if you've used a wash off cleanser.

Even oily skins need a light moisturiser. Look for one that says 'non-comedogenic' and 'oil free'. Some new light moisturisers also have a mattefying effect which stops your skin from getting oily so quickly. A light moisturising gel is perfect.

Explaining the Science: Non-comedogenic just means there is nothing in the moisturiser that will block up your pores. Oil free means exactly that, there's no oil in the moisturiser and mattefying means that it will keep your skin matte – these often have some sort of microsponges, silica or clay added to soak up excess oil.

skincare for normal/dry skin

❋ Dry skin needs some tender loving care to look its best. The regime you adopt now will help look after your skin in years to come. This is most important with dry skin as it ages the fastest.

❋ You can still use a wash off cleanser if you like the feel of water on your skin, but a creamy cleanser is better. Pour a small amount on to the back of your hand to warm the product and the massage onto your face. Now wipe off gently with cotton wool pads.

❋ If you want to get rid of every trace of cleanser, you could use a gentle toner. Soak a cotton wool pad in the toner and sweep across your skin. Never use a toner that includes alcohol – it is so dehydrating! Look for something containing rosewater or just use lukewarm tap water.

❋ Dry skin needs a richer moisturiser than oily skin. Use something that says it is 'hydrating' and has been formulated especially for dry skin. If your skin feels especially tight in a morning, try using a night cream.

❋ Explaining the Science: Hydrating just means that the moisturiser makes sure your skin is getting extra moisture – like when you drink extra water to hydrate your body!

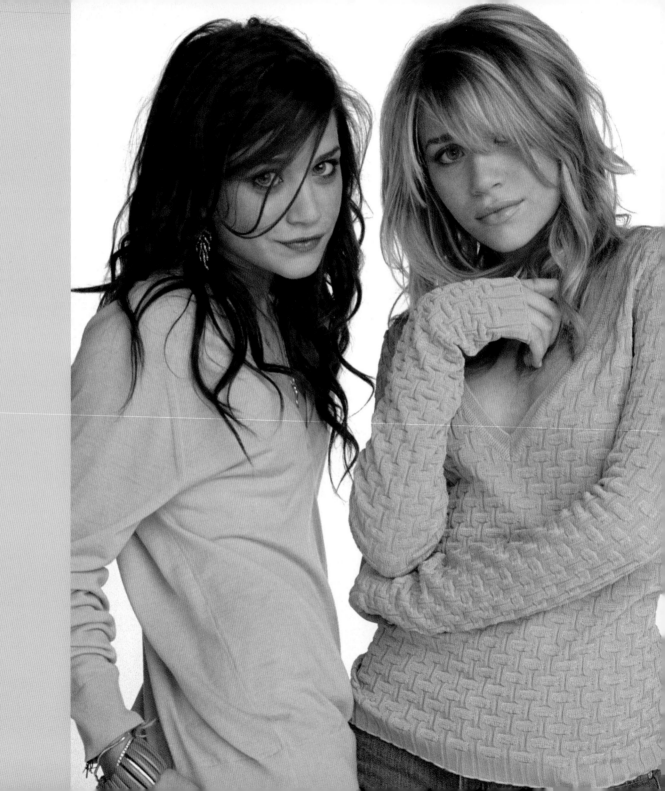

what products do you really need?

❋ Young skin doesn't really need all that many products. Just something to keep your complexion clean and moisturised and a weekly face mask.

❋ Normal to Oily Skin – wash off cleansing gel, oil-free moisturiser and a clay-based face mask.

❋ Normal to Dry skin – creamy cleansing lotion, cotton wool pads, gentle toner/warm water, moisturising cream and a hydrating face mask.

❋ The latest ready-to-use, wet cleansing cloths on the market might be super convenient but they aren't the best thing for your skin. Keep a pack handy for sleepovers and late nights but always try and remove your make-up properly. The cleansing cloths can leave a residue on your skin and don't always clean deep down.

❋ If you wear a lot of eye make-up, you might want to invest in a special eye make-up remover and eye cream. Rubbing at the delicate eye area will make it age more quickly (but not for a long time yet!) and prevention is always better than the cure!

homemade heaven

It's easy to find some skin treats around the house, without going out and spending a fortune. Try these homemade recipes for glowing skin, shiny hair and relaxed eyes.

cucumber eye mask

Slice a cucumber into 5 millimetre thick slices, pop them on your eyes and relax! The scientific explanation for this is that cucumbers contain ascorbic acid and caffeic acid, both of which prevent water retention which is the main cause of puffy eyes.

honey facial – dry skin

Beat an egg yolk with a fork, add a teaspoon of olive oil and blend well. Then add a tablespoon of clear honey and blend again. Gently rub this onto your face avoiding your eyes and leave for 15 minutes. Rinse off and pat dry.

strawberry facial – oily skin

Crush about ten strawberries and 1/4 of a cup of cornstarch together to make a paste. Once the paste is smooth, apply to your face. Leave for 20 minutes then rinse and pat your skin dry.

the dreaded zit

❋ Here's the facts – no-one wants zits and almost everyone has them! They're an unpleasant fact of life and a very real part of being a teenager, although acne can strike at any age. Wouldn't you rather have a few spots now than a breakout when you're 30?

❋ Never pick a spot – no matter how tempting. What's worse? A red zit for a week or a scar for a lifetime?

❋ Most people agree what you eat doesn't directly result in zits, but rather that blemishes are caused by hormones, and guess what? Your hormones are up and down like a rollercoaster right now. But while no one food is the cause of bad skin, a healthy diet can help prevent outbreaks.

❋ Try using a topical spot cream from the chemist and a medicated concealer stick. If your skin is really getting you down, go to your doctor. They won't laugh at you, they probably had problem skin when they were your age. There are lots of treatments for acne these days and your doctor should be able to help.

sunny days

* Most people love the sun but all that time spent sunbathing with your buddies can be really bad for your skin if you're not wearing sun cream. Did you know that 99% of the wrinkles you will get in your life are caused by exposure to the sun?

* It's important to ALWAYS wear a high SPF (sun protection factor) on your face, neck and hands – at least SPF 15 – all year round not just on holiday. Most good moisturisers and foundations have an SPF built in but try and have a tube handy (plus putting on sun cream always reminds you of your holidays!)

* SPFs relate to the time you can spend in the sun. It is math, but it's easy! If your skin usually burns in ten minutes, if you wear a sun cream with an SPF of 15, you can stay out 15 times longer i.e. 150 minutes before you need to reapply your sun cream. The higher the SPF, the longer you can stay in the sun.

* And never forget your shades and big hat during the hottest times of the day!

all over gorgeous

✳ Think about how much hard work your skin does for you. It's always there, being rubbed against clothes, being covered in make-up, going from hot bath to cold outdoors and then into dry air conditioning. Don't you think it deserves a treat now and again?

✳ We all think to exfoliate and moisturise our hands and faces but you must never forget your body. Legs get especially dry and often need intensive moisturiser, especially in winter when they're tucked away in jeans and don't get any fresh air.

✳ To make an effective exfoliator at home, mix a handful of sea salt with three glugs of olive oil. Now take your mixture into the shower and rub it gently over your legs, arms, bottom and back. Avoid your front as the skin can be more delicate. Once you've rinsed off, smother yourself in moisturiser – it really doesn't have to be expensive, just rich and easily absorbed.

✳ For a real hand or toenail treat, before bed, rub lots of hand cream into your hands and feet, then slip on a pair of cotton socks. In the morning, your hands and feet will be super soft!

perfect nails

❊ Your nails say a lot about you, so try not to bite them. It's a really bad habit and not at all good for your nails or your teeth!

❊ If you don't want long, manicured nails, trim them every week and keep them in check with an emery board. A coat of clear polish will keep them looking nice.

❊ If you like looking after your nails, try and devote and hour a week to a DIY manicure. Start by removing any polish you might have on already, then shape your nails with an emery board.

❊ Next, use a clear base coat to protect your nails – you don't want them to turn yellow! Now paint with your chosen colour and then finish off with a top coat. Even fast drying polishes really need an hour to completely harden – why not tie-in your manicure with your favourite TV show? The perfect excuse to sit in front of the TV!

❊ Nail polish is an area where you can really show off your personality and use lots of different colours. Don't spend a lot of money on designer brands, you change your nail looks so often it isn't worth it.

easy eyebrows

✳ Did you ever really look at your eyebrows? Why do we even have them when we spend so much time plucking them? Well, according to scientists, it's to keep rain and sweat out of our eyes (yuck!).

✳ One thing's for sure, your eyebrows really frame your face and plucking them can make your features stand out more. Before you go crazy with the tweezers, talk to your mum – she might not be happy about you plucking your eyebrows yet!

✳ Once you've got the OK, there are some simple rules. Hold a pencil straight up alongside your nose so it touches your eyebrow. Anything between the tip of the pencil and your other eyebrow can be plucked, now do the same on the other side.

✳ Now look at the main body of your eyebrow – anything underneath the main part can be plucked. Try colouring the hairs you're planning to pluck with a white eye pencil – this should give you a good idea of how your eyebrows will look afterwards.

✳ The most important rules are only to pluck one hair at a time, NEVER pluck from above your brow line and take a look at both your brows in the mirror after you've plucked each hair to ensure they're balanced and that you're not plucking too much.

exercise = healthy skin

❄ As well as avoiding the sun, eating lots of fruit and drinking lots of water, one of the best things for your skin is exercise. Once your heart rate is up, your blood pumps faster making your skin glowy. Sweating during exercise also helps get rid of nasty toxins that build up in the skin.

❄ There are a million different types of exercise to try – why not give a few of these a go and see which one you prefer?

❄ Swimming – works every muscle in your body and, as long as you take a shower to get rid of the chlorine, is great for your skin!

❄ Yoga – all that bending and stretching can really get your heart rate up without you even noticing. Plus it's good for posture and balance.

❄ Dancing – any kind of dancing as long as you keep it up for thirty minutes at a time! Try Swing dancing; it's great fun and you'll make lots of friends at classes.

❄ Martial Arts – disciplines like Tae Kwon Do and Karate aren't just for boys! And as well as exercising, you're learning some kick-butt moves which every girl should know.

home spa

Don't you just hate it when all your friends have plans for the weekend and you have nothing to do? Well, you could always use that spare time to set up your own home spa... Remember to ask permission first – the family bathroom is about to become your private pampering sanctuary!

You'll need a couple of hours for the top to-toe-treatment. Start by tying your hair back and exfoliating your face. Use a gentle scrub and avoid your eyes where the skin is most delicate. Once you've rinsed off the scrub and patted your skin dry, wash your hair with a detoxifying shampoo. This removes any product build-up in your scalp.

Now your face and hair are squeaky clean, run a lovely, warm bath. Use a bath oil rather than

bubbles as it's more moisturising. Before you hop in, smooth on a hydrating face pack and a deep conditioning hair treatment. The steam from your bath will help them work better.

Don't stay in the tub too long – your skin will actually start to dry out! After about fifteen to twenty minutes, jump out and wash off your face and hair treats. Now towel off, then smother yourself with a rich moisturiser.

If you've got time, now is a great time to pluck your eyebrows, as your pores are open from the steamy bath. If you want to give yourself a manicure and pedicure, exfoliate and moisturise now, but wait a while before you file your nails, they are too soft straight after a bath.

your perfume

✻ Finding your perfect perfume is such a fun and personal adventure. Some girls find one scent in their teens and stick with it for life, as a signature scent. Other girls like to collect a whole dresser full of beautiful perfume bottles so the have a scent for every occasion. The most important thing to remember is to choose a perfume that you love!

✻ Lots of department stores give away testers of their new perfumes – it's great way to try new scents. Also, look out for perfume strips in magazines. Cut these out and pop them in your underwear draw – mmm, scented smalls!

✻ The best way to make your perfume last all day is to layer the scent by washing in the shower gel, moisturising with the body lotion and then spraying on perfume. This can be a bit pricey, so a good way to layer up is to buy unscented body oil, add a few drops of your perfume and then use the oil as a bath oil and a body moisturiser!

✳ If you really like a certain scent on someone else, test it on yourself before you buy. Everyone's skin is different and can make the final scent of a perfume different. If a perfume smells very heavy on you, there might be a lighter version of the same scent like Angel/Angel Innocent or Chanel Coco/Coco Madamoiselle. Just ask at the counter!

top ten tips

These are your top ten, never forget them, fail safe beauty tips:

1. Always wear sunscreen, it's the most important product you'll ever use on your skin.

2. Cleanse and moisturise daily – get into the right routine morning and night.

3. If you don't eat right or get enough exercise, your skin won't look great no matter how many swanky products you use.

4. Don't overload your skin – you don't need tonnes of creams, lotions and potions. Keep it simple.

5. Make sure you're using the right products for you. If you use heavy creams on oily skin, you will make your problems worse.

6. Never pick a spot! Unless you really want an unsightly scar.

7. Always take your make-up off at the end of the day. No-one looks good with panda eyes!

8. Less is more when plucking your eyebrows. Ask a good friend or your mum to advise you while you're plucking.

9. Your perfume should reflect your personality – don't buy the one with the best advert!

10. Prevention is always better than the cure – a good beauty regime now will take years off you in the future.

2 make-up makeover

Make-up is great. It's fun, it's pretty inexpensive and it can make us look great. But in most cases, less really is more. Do you really need sixteen eyeliners? And how many pink lipsticks can one girl wear? And did you know make-up can go off? Ewww.

This section looks at what make-up you need on a day-to-day basis, how much you really need to spend and how long until it needs replacing.

Once you've got the basics, then you can start looking at the fun stuff. We've broken everything down into Must-Haves, Good to Have and Just for Fun – but hey, if you need glitter eyeliner to get through the day, who are we to tell you otherwise?!

must-haves

❖ These are really the basic building blocks of your beauty case. Once you've got all these basics, you will be able to build a great look for any occasion.

❖ Must-Haves are also the products it's worth spending the most money on because you'll wear them the most often. That's not to say head straight to your closest designer beauty hall and clear out the cosmetics counter, but shop around for these products; they shouldn't be impulse buys.

❖ If you're going to put something on your face every day, make sure it's right for you – it should never irritate your skin and should be exactly the right shade.

foundation

❖ Once you've found the perfect foundation, everything else seems so much easier! The perfect shade should blend seamlessly into your skin and leave no tell tale tidemarks on your jawline. It's easiest to use your fingers to apply foundation but you could use a special brush or sponge.

❖ Always try foundation on your skin before you buy – ask the store for a sample or use a tester. It's no good trying foundation on the back of your hand as your skintone is completely different.

Yellow-based foundations look most natural. Avoid anything too pink.

❖ Be prepared and take a pocket mirror and some face wipes in your handbag so you can wipe away any bad matches and check the different shades in daylight.

❖ Younger skins don't need a heavy foundation. They can make you look very 'done up' and much older than you are.

❖ There are lots of different kinds of foundation but it's easy to work out which one is for you:

Tinted moisturiser – this is very sheer and just adds a little colour to your skin. Best for girls who only need a little help evening out their skintone.

Fluid foundation – a little heavier than tinted moisturiser, this foundation will give you better coverage but is still light and easy to blend.

Cream foundation – best for older women and girls with very dry skin, this foundation can feel very heavy.

Mousse foundation – great for young skins that need good coverage, this foundation feels light and airy but gives plenty of coverage.

Cream-to-Powder foundation – this is a heavier foundation that smooths on like a cream but turns to a powder finish on the skin.

concealer

❖ There are lots of kinds of concealers for blemishes, spots, under your eyes and even for birthmarks. The easiest kind to use comes in a tube, like lipstick, and you can apply it straight onto your skin or use a little brush.

❖ Have you ever seen a green concealer and wondered what it is? Well, it's colour-correcting make-up. If you apply a green concealer on top of a red spot, the green neautralises the red, making it less noticeable!

❖ Some concealers are medicated which are great if you have a problem with spots as they can cover up and dry the zit out at the same time.

❖ Covering up a spot can often make it look worse than if you just leave it alone. Start by washing your face, moisturising and applying your foundation.

❖ Now apply a tiny bit of concealer onto your spot and blend it outwards. Repeat once or twice until it's covered up. There shouldn't be too much concealer around the spot or it will be very noticeable.

❖ Set with loose powder – there! Now you're ready to face the world.

pressed powder

❖ Pressed powder really is your best friend. It fits into your handbag, sets your make-up and is perfect for little touch ups when you're on the go. The best compacts have an applicator sponge or a velvet puff included and should have a mirror inside the lid.

❖ As with most make-up, you have to know when enough is enough – pressed powder should only be applied to your t-zone or oily areas of skin. Young skin should look gorgeous and glowing, too much powder will make it look dry and crepey.

❖ Begin by applying your foundation and concealer as usual then dab your sponge/puff into your pressed powder. Now stroke the applicator across your forehead, down your nose and across your chin and jaw line. Your skin should look velvet soft but still have a natural glow.

lip gloss

❖   There are a million lip products on the market but the easiest to wear and most fun to apply is lip gloss. Glosses come in every colour you can imagine, some are sheer, some are dense, some have sparkles and some are flavoured – yum!

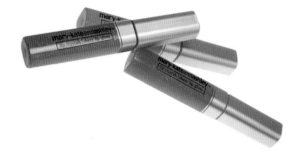

❖   Glosses are a good way to try out new colours as they aren't as dense as lipsticks and won't stain your lips with colour if you change your mind. If you're trying out a bright red or a rich berry colour for the first time, go for a gloss first. If you like the colour, you can always use the gloss in the daytime or over the top of your lipstick to make it glossier.

❖ The easiest glosses to use, and carry around in your pocket, come in handy little tubes. Just unscrew the top, squeeze the tube and smooth onto your lips.

❖ For a more dramatic colour, a lip gloss tube with a wand is perfect as it gives you more control over your application.

❖ Rollerball glosses tend to be a little thinner than tubes or wands but they are so much fun and really easy to apply! A perfect 'my first lipgloss'.

mascara

❖ Heaps of girls pick mascara as their desert island beauty product. By colouring your lashes, mascara really frames your face, makes your eyes look more dramatic and finishes off the rest of your look.

❖ Mascara can be a little scary to apply the first time but once you've got the hang of it, you'll be able to whip out the wand and coat your lashes in no time! The easiest trick to try the first few times you apply mascara is to wipe almost all the colour from the wand with a tissue before you comb through your lashes. There will still be enough mascara on the wand to colour your lashes but not enough to clump. It should also dry quicker and be less likely to run.

❖ There are lots of different kinds of mascara – thickening, lengthening, glossy and more. There's no need to go for a false lash look for every day, so play it safe with a natural, glossy formula and try out the lengthening and thickening formulas for the evening.

❖ If you have dark hair and dark eyelashes, you can use black mascara but if you have blonde or red hair, stick with brown mascara – it just looks more natural.

blusher

❖ Blusher can be a subtle way of emphasising the shape of your face as well as creating some really sweet looks. Before you start applying colour, decide which formula is best for you – powder or cream.

❖ If your skin is very dry, you might be better with a cream blusher, which glides on easily. If you have normal to oily skin, go for a powder blush. Cream blushers can be applied with a sponge or your fingers, powder blusher with a large brush.

❖ For a natural look, apply your blusher to the apples of your cheeks – the parts that round out when you smile – and blend outwards. Start with a tiny amount and build the colour up. It's easier to apply more than to have to take off all your make-up and start again.

neutral eyeshadow

❖   Your eyes are one of the easiest features to play up and look great with just a little definition. Whether you have blue, green or brown eyes, a light brown shadow, blended along your lash line, will make your eyes sparkle. A silvery brown will work best, reddy browns will make your eyes look red and sore.

❖   Again, you can use cream or powder formulations but powder shadow usually lasts longer. Prep your eyelids with foundation and pressed powder, then dip the tip of a small eyeshadow brush into your eye colour and stroke lightly onto your eyelid. Keep close to your lash line and don't take the colour any further up than your crease.

❖   Other shades that look good on all eye colours are cream, dove grey and soft lilac. A light wash of any of these colours is great for daytime and the grey and brown can be built up for a more dramatic night time look.

nice to have

❖ Once you've got your Must-Haves, you can easily build a basic look for the daytime. It's important to get your technique right with these products before moving on to more products.

❖ Once you've got your day face perfected, it's time to play around with some more products. Nice to Have products will make your every day make-up case that tiny bit more fun and give you more choice in your everyday look.

❖ Most of them work with your Must-Have make-up whereas others can be substituted for a change. Use loose powder at home and keep your pressed powder in your handbag, lipstick can be used on its own or under lipgloss and light reflecting concealer works with your regular stick concealer. Others are fun additions, like nail colour and highlighters.

loose powder

❖ Loose powder works in the same way as pressed powder but gives a more natural look. It generally comes in a large pot and is applied with a velvet puff or a large fluffy brush – the bigger the better!

❖ Look for the word 'translucent' (this means see through) on the label and always test the colour in the same way as foundation before you buy. Apply your foundation and concealer as usual and then use your velvet puff to stroke the loose powder onto your skin. Then use your large powder brush and brush away any excess powder.

❖ Loose powder can also be dusted underneath your eyes before applying coloured eye shadows. If any shadow falls under your eye, you can just brush it away without making a mess of the rest of your make-up. Also look out for powders that include light reflecting particles to stop your skin looking too dry and powdery.

lipstick

❖ Lipstick hasn't been too popular lately. A lot of people think it's too thick, drying and old fashioned – something your mother wears. But in the last few years, lipsticks have really changed. They're a great way of using dramatic colour on your mouth and good lipsticks shouldn't smudge or need to be reapplied every time you have a drink.

❖ Almost all make-up brands have a sheer version of their colours. They should be light, sparkly and easy to apply, almost a cross between a gloss and a full lipstick. These are a perfect way of trying out new colours or just for daytime.

❖ For evenings and party looks, you might want a more dramatic look so you'll need a deeper colour. Look for a rich, creamy formulation that won't dry out your lips. You can always add a slick of gloss over the top if you think the look is too harsh.

❖ Alternatively, try one of the new long lasting lip colours that you paint onto your lips with a wand. Once the colour has dried, you apply a gloss topcoat whenever your lips start to feel dry. The colour should last all day without touch-ups.

lip balms

❖ Lip balms are the best. Not only are they moisturising, they can add a little colour and sparkle and are great to keep in your pocket, your handbag, your desk and anywhere else you might need one. Collecting lip balms can be totally addictive!

❖ Your lips have fewer natural moisturisers than any other part of your body so they need extra help. There are hundreds of kinds of lip balm, solid sticks you just rub on, pots of balm that you apply with your finger or a brush, tubes of gel, or even simple tins of petroleum jelly. Balms with natural ingredients like shea or cocoa butter are great but any kind of balm will work well. As silly as it sounds, try not to apply too often or your lips might forget they need to moisturise themselves and dry out completely.

❖ If you're just looking for something to pop in your pocket, then go for a stick lip balm that's either colourless or lightly tinted.

Before you buy a lip balm, remember to check if it has a UV filter to protect your lips from the sun.

lip liner

❖ Lip liner really helps finish a polished look but you have to be really careful not to overdo the look. The key thing to remember is never to wear lip liner alone and never use a darker shade than the lip colour you're planning to wear. If in doubt go for a neutral colour in a tawny pink shade that matches your natural lip colour.

❖ Moisturise your lips before applying the liner and then careful trace the outline of your lips with the pencil. Round of the tip before you start and use light feathery stokes, rather than a hard outline. This will be easier to blend.

❖ Now take your lip brush and lip colour and fill in the outline. Once your lips are fully coloured, press them against a single piece of tissue paper and dust with translucent powder. Now apply another layer of lip colour. Your lip liner should help your lip colour look neat and polished but not too obvious. If you can still see the liner, blend the two colours with your lip brush.

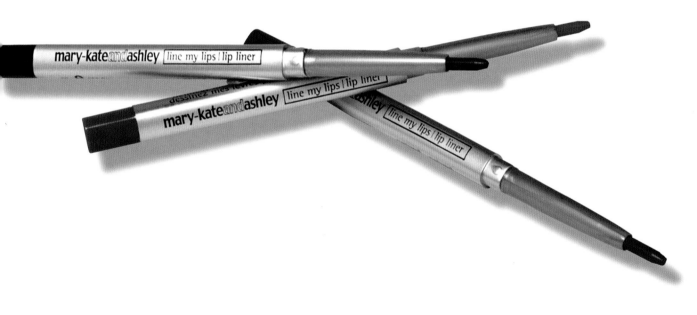

highlighter

❖ Highlighter is a great way to emphasise your best features. Look for either a fluid or a cream highlighter so that you can control exactly wear you apply it and always remember to blend! If you have a warm skin tone, look for a golden highlighter whereas pale skin tones look best with a pinky-silvery highlighter.

❖ For a luminous daytime look, blend a drop of fluid highlighter into your everyday foundation. Mix in well and then apply as usual, you'll look fresh and glowy. Finish up with a touch of pressed powder and your nose and chin – the look should be fresh not greasy. Remember not to overdo it.

❖ For an evening look, use a regular base then add highlighter to the tops of your cheekbones. Start with two small dots and blend upward. Now add a small dot underneath each eyebrow to open up your eyes and a small dot on the cupid's bow of your top lip. This should make you face look bright and open and emphasise all your best features!

coloured eyeshadows

❖ Coloured eyeshadows are a fun way to try out new shades. Start with a neutral base of foundation and loose powder, then use a small, rounded brush to apply your base colour. Stick to easy to wear colours and keep the formulations sheer, light and easy to blend.

❖ Colours for warm skin tones – Anything with a warm, orangey base colour such as warm browns, golds, khaki, bright yellow, copper, bronze.

❖ Colours for cool skin tones – Anything with a blue base colour – ice blue, lavender, silver, turquoise, mint green, taupe.

sheer nail polish

❖ Nail polish is fun but it's important to take care of your nails. Moisturise your hands and nails regularly and always remove your polish once it starts to chip.

❖ For every day, light sheer colours are best. Pastel pinks, sparkly whites and cool creams look good with all outfits. Keep your nails short and rounded and always apply a base coat.

❖ Start your manicure by removing any polish you might already be wearing and filing your nails into a neat shape. Now apply your base coat and give it five minutes to dry. The best way to apply the colour is to start with a single stripe in the centre of your nail, followed by two thinner stripes on either side. Try not to run the polish right to the edges of the nail for a neater finish. A fast-drying topcoat will stop your polish from chipping and keep it extra glossy.

light diffusing concealer

❖ If you have dark circles under your eyes, you might want to cover them up. Lots of people have dark circles and they can be caused by lots of things: lack of sleep, dehydration or they can even be hereditary.

❖ Use a light-reflecting concealer (that means it reflects the light from under your eyes, making them look sparklier) that often comes in a pen. Dot the fluid lightly under your eye and blend gently with your ring finger. Never pull and tug at the skin around your eyes, as it's very delicate.

❖ You can also use light reflecting concealer as a subtle highlighter by dotting it under your eyebrows, above your top lip. You can brighten up the centre of your face by using light reflecting concealer around your nose to even out your skin tone.

just for fun

❖ Just for Fun items are the bits and pieces in your make-up box that will make your beauty kit truly unique. Do you look fab in aubergine eyeliner? You won't know until you try. How about a flash of blue mascara? Or a block of green eyeshadow?

❖ OK, so a block of green eyeshadow won't suit everyone but for olive skins and the very bold, it can look amazing.

❖ Even though this section is where you get to break all the rules and have fun, always remember less is more. Hot pink eyeshadow won't look good teamed with bright green eyeliner and cheeks smeared with glitter gel. Honestly, you're not going to get away with that unless you're on the catwalk, but do try things out. That's the best thing about make-up – it all washes off and you can change it every day, so have fun!

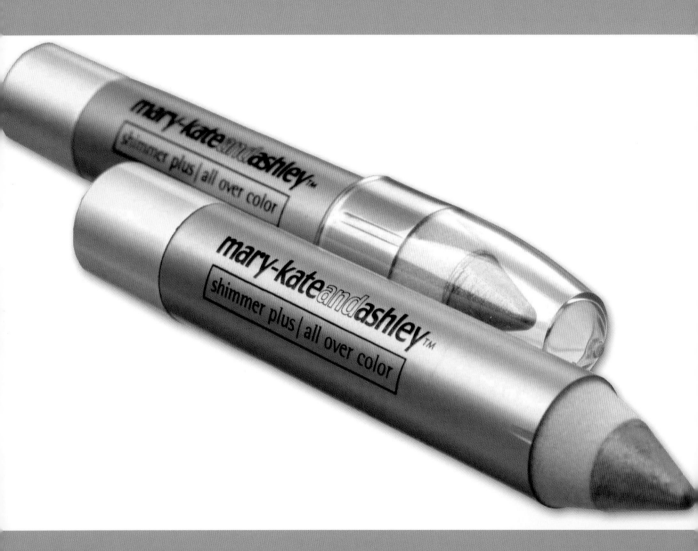

coloured eyeliner

❖ Eyeliner comes in many different shapes and sizes. Go with liquid for a vivid colour and pencil if you want to smudge and look a little subtler. Navy blue or aubergine makes a fun change from black, brown or grey and gives a softer look for every day if you decide eyeliner is for you.

❖ For a fun punk princess look, grab a black kohl pencil, soften the tip until it's rounded and lightly line all the way around your eyes. Keep close to the eyelashes or you'll look like you have a black eye – now smudge outwards. Beautiful! For a cleaner look, use liquid liner and rest your elbow on a flat surface as you line to avoid the dreaded eyeliner shakes.

❖ A strong eyeliner look is great with a bare face, so go easy on the rest of your look. Foundation, lip balm or clear gloss and a healthy cheek colour are all you need. And don't forget to finish off the look with lashings of mascara to make your eyes pop.

funky eyeshadows

❖ Coloured eyeshadows are a really fun way to try out a signature look but bear in mind, some skin tones do not suit certain colours no matter how much you love them. Warm and olive skin tones look best in warm colours while cool skin tones look

better in icier shades. The easiest way to find your most complementary colours is to check out the colour wheel and choose the colour opposite your own eye colour. This will make your eye colour stand out.

❖ You might not believe it but orangey-browns make blue eyes stand out across a room, while green eyes look amazing paired with a violet colour, smudged all the way around the eye. Brown eyes are lucky and work with lots of different colours so experiment and see what works best for you.

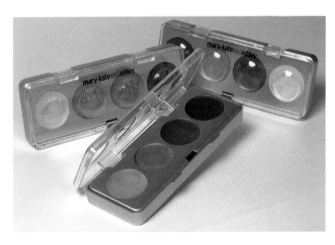

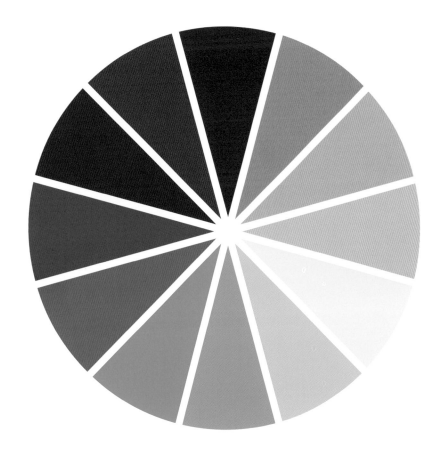

❖ When choosing metallics, stick to gold and bronze for warm skin tones and silvery pearls for cool – anything else will make you look ill rather than glam. Also, never wear more than one colour at a time – it was so cool in the 80s to blend a blue up into a pink, but is it the 80s anymore? No. Keep it clean, close to your lash line and one colour at a time, people!

glitter

❖ Glitter is so much fun and comes in a million different shades and formulas. Iridescent glitter looks great on everyone dotted on your cheekbones or on your eyelids. If you're wearing glitter on your cheekbones, try not to pile on too much or you'll just look weird instead of ready to party.

❖ For a really striking party look, line your lash line with petroleum jelly and then dab a thin line of glitter along until it sticks. Now coat your lashes with mascara and apply a sparkly lip gloss.

Before you put anything near your eyes, check that it's safe and if you wear contacts, don't even try this. Glitter stuck to a contact lens is both painful and damaging so stick with a metallic silver or gold liner instead.

❖ If you don't want to put glitter on your face (it's too harsh for some sensitive skins) why not try a glitter nail polish or a glitter spray for your hair? If you don't have glitter nail polish you can always make your own. Paint your nails with a sheer base colour and sprinkle each nail with a fine glitter, then finish with a clear top coat.

bright nail polish

❖ Like bright eyeshadows, bright nail polishes are a great way of being individual but remember, some schools don't like you to wear nail colour so save it for holidays and special occasions. If you are going to wear bright colours, always wear a base coat to stop your nails from staining.

❖ If you're feeling all punk pop, then by all means try a dark polish but black is a really tricky one to get rid of, so make sure you use two coats of base before you apply. Why not go for a dark sparkly blue or a midnight purple instead. Much cooler. If you're going dark, keep your nails short and rounded otherwise you're in danger of looking like a vampire.

❖ Milkshake colours look really cool – baby blues, pastel pinks and pale violets and go with most outfits but remember how easily fingernail polish chips. If in doubt, just paint your tootsies and show off in a pair of cute flip-flops.

hair stylers

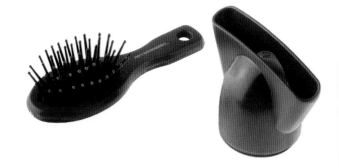

Playing with make-up is a really good way of changing your look but another great and temporary way is to use hair stylers! Before you start using heated appliances on your hair, always make sure it is completely dry or you won't get an even end result. Section off your hair and point your hairdryer downwards for extra shiny hair.

Straighteners can be much more versatile than you think. As well as creating sophisticated, poker straight locks, they can be used to create waves, body and shape. Instead of pulling them straight down your hair, try curling it under at the end to give a bob bounce. If your hair is long, section it off and curl it around your straighteners for loose waves.

❖ Curling tongs might seem old fashioned but they give a great result without the drastic action of perming! You can create tight ringlets, all over loose angel waves or just curl small sections of hair to create interesting texture. If you have long hair, try pinning back the front sections and curling a few strands around your face for a pretty, summery look.

tools of the trade
– brushes

Today's make-up is really easy to apply with your fingers but there are still a few brushes that are important additions to your make-up collection:

Powder blush – this should be as big and fluffy a brush as you can find. It's for dusting away the excess pressed powder left behind by your puff and should give your skin a finished, velvety look.

Blusher brush – this should be fairly large and rounded with a long handle to help you get an even flush of colour.

Eyeliner brush – an eyeliner brush is great if you're not confident with liquid liner. Go for a long handled, flat, angled brush that you can press along your eyeliner and blend, or sweep for a more solid line.

Eyeshadow brush – eyeshadows are easy to apply with your fingers but sometimes you need the control of a brush. You'll need one brush with a rounded, fairly full head for base colour and another that is smaller for contouring.

Lipbrush – again, not a necessity but for some reason, lipstick just seems to stay on for longer when you use a brush. It's a mystery to all of us...

tools of the trade
– accessories

Like the brushes, none of these things will make or break your beauty regime but they will make looking good that little bit easier.

Eyelash curlers – go for metal or plastic but make sure they have a good rubber grip in the clamps. Without this you'll be damaging your lashes. Don't curl more than once a day and never pull – you might stress your lashes and they'll all fall out!

Foundation sponges – some people don't like to blend foundation with their fingers, even though your body heat helps the make-up melt more naturally into your skin. If you want to try a more polished look, use a wedged sponge. Remember to always wash them out with a mild face wash.

Tweezers – this is something that is worth investing in. Look for a long handled pair of tweezers that will give you better control. They should also have sharp, slanted ends to help you grab one lash at a time.

Tissues and cotton buds – for application and quick clean-ups! Use cotton buds to clear up mascara smudges or to apply eyeliner, and always have tissues handy to wipe excess make-up from applicators and to blot your lips!

make-up S.O.S

❖ Here are some handy hints to help resolve some make-up emergencies.

❖ It's a nightmare when your mascara smudges and an awful lot of hard work to take all your make-up off and start from scratch. Try dotting a cotton bud with foundation and wiping away the smudge.

❖ If you've applied too much blusher, try toning down the colour with a dab of loose powder.

❖ If you've got tide marks on your jaw line, then your foundation is too dark for you. To lighten your foundation, mix in a little of your regular moisturiser before you apply.

❖ To avoid lipstick on the teeth, blot and pop a finger in your mouth and pull it out. You might look crazy doing it but it will avoid embarrassing moments later on.

double duty beauty

❖ There are heaps of products that work in more than one way which will save you time and money. Plus it's easier to carry one product than three!

❖ Look for colour products that work on your lips, cheeks and eyes for a co-ordinated look. Not only are they quick and easy but you'll know that all your make-up matches.

❖ If you're using a silvery eyeshadow or liner, why not double it up as a highlighter? Dot it along your cheekbones and brow bones and blend well. You can also use your light diffusing concealer as a highlighter for a more subtle effect.

❖ For quick and easy eyeliner, dampen an eyeliner brush, dip it in your eyeshadow and line your lashes.

❖ Want shimmery skin? Mix a little bit of your highlighter in with your regular body lotion and apply all over for extra sparkle.

don't do it!

We're all about experimenting with make-up to come up with new looks but there are a few easy mistakes you can avoid.

Beauty rule #1
You can play up your eyes, lips or cheeks but never all three at once. **Strong lips + natural lips + blush** or **Strong lips + natural blush + mascara** or **Glittery cheeks + clear glossed lips + brown/black mascara.**

Beauty rule #2
Fresh and natural always looks better than overdone – if in doubt, just go simple touch of blusher, powder on your forehead, nose and chin and a touch of lip gloss.

Beauty rule #3
Never, ever match your eyeshadow to your clothes – it's not co-ordination, it's just wrong. Match your colours to your mood, to your favourite painting or picture in a magazine. There are heaps of places to find colour inspiration without turning to what's on your back.

Beauty rule #4
There's a time and place for everything. Electric blue eyeshadow with ruby

red lips might look amazing in the pages of your favourite magazine but they aren't going to look great in geography at 10.00am on a Tuesday morning,

3 hot hair

Hot Hair is all about making the most of your mop. It's a fact that girls with poker straight hair dream about their friend's curly locks, and the curly girls will fry their hair with straighteners in an attempt to copy their straight haired friends.

Well, there's good news and there's bad news. If you've got straight hair, it's never going to be permanently curly and if you're a curly girl, it's never going to be totally straight. This chapter will show you how to make the most of what you've got and how to achieve some temporary transformations.

Just like your skin, your hair needs to be in tip top condition before you start colouring or playing with heated stylers. Imagine how you would feel in a red hot room without a drink of water – that's your unconditioned hair being tortured with heated styling tongs!

taking care of your hair

❀ Your hair is just as delicate as your skin and needs a lot of TLC. Think about how often you run your brush through it, pull it up into a ponytail, and rub it with a towel – ouch! And that's without thinking about hairdryers, curlers, straightners, etc.

❀ Start washing your hair with a gentle shampoo and try not to wash more than every other day. Next condition with the right formula for your hair – is your hair light and flyaway, thick and dry or does it get greasy quickly? Try not to use 2-in-1 formulations. These often include silicone which just coats your hair rather than conditions.

❀ Try and let your hair dry naturally as often as possible. It really is the best way for your hair to recuperate and look its best. Save your straightening and curling irons for special occasions.

choosing a stylist

✻ When you were younger, you probably didn't have much of a say in who cut your hair but when the time comes to choose your stylist, choose carefully! The first thing to do is to speak to friends who have great hair and find out who cuts it. Next, have a look at some magazines and look for styles you like. Once you've got a collection of looks, take them along to a couple of stylists recommended by your friends.

✻ Once you've chatted for ten minutes you'll soon know who you want to cut your hair. The right stylist will make you feel at ease and discuss the styles you've brought in honestly. No-one

should promise to make you look exactly like the girl in the photo but they should suggest ways to tailor the look to your hair type and face shape. Don't stick around if the stylist makes you feel uncomfortable or is rude; there are plenty of hair stylists in the world.

❋ It's generally true that the longer you stick with a good stylist, the better your hair will look. As the stylist gets to know your personality and your style, they will be able to suggest more styles for your hair. For example, you might love swimming but not mention it to your hair stylist for the first couple of visits. But when you do mention it, a good stylist might suggest a shorter style that's easier to take care of out of the pool.

choosing a style

✿ Choosing a hairstyle depends on lots of things – your personal style, your face shape, your hobbies – so have a look at lots of magazines and the suggestions on the next few pages, then take your ideas along to discuss with your stylist.

Round face: Build height into your style with layers and emphasise those cheekbones.

✿

Long face: A fringe shortens your face and gives it more shape.

✿

Heart-shaped face: A cute pixie crop or lots of layers flatters you.

✿

Oval face: Oval faces can try any styles so go for it and experiment!

style to suit you
– long

❀ Long hair is pretty, feminine and romantic but it's also the trickiest of all hairstyles to look after. Be prepared for a lot of conditioning and hours spent blow-drying. You're going to need strong arms to hold up that hairdryer, girl!

❀ Long styles can be worn up or down and work some really dramatic looks. Ask your stylist to cut in layers – it will help your hair look thicker and healthier and make-it easier for you to look after.

style to suit you
– medium

✼ Medium length hair is the most versatile length you can choose. As long as it touches your shoulders, you can wear it up as well as down, curly or straight and it's much easier to look after than long hair.

✼ If you've got long hair and you're thinking about getting the chop, live with a mid-length style for a few months before going all the way, then it won't be such a shock to the system.

style to suit you
– short

❉ Short hair is incredibly easy to look after and looks cool and modern but be prepared for regular trips to the stylist as short styles need a trim every four to six weeks to keep them looking perfect.

❉ Long bangs frame your face and help camouflage a big forehead. Whether you go for a pixie crop or keep some length, a short crop will draw all attention to your face.

❉ We had shorter hair when we were younger. It's perfect if you're always running around with no time for a high maintenance style, like we were!

choosing a colour

❀ Changing your hair colour is a lot of fun and lets you try out a whole new look without buying a whole new wardrobe or chopping off all your hair. Before you do anything at all to the colour of your hair, check with your parents – a lot of colourants are permanent and you should never do anything permanent without getting permission first.

❀ Professional colouring can be very expensive but if you're planning something drastic like bleaching, you must get it done at a salon. The best advice is to play it safe and start with a wash in/ wash out colourant that you can try at home.

Highlights/Lowlights – If you love the way your hair looks after a week in the sun, you might want to try highlights. This is when you lighten small sections of hair all over your head, but be careful because highlights are permanent. If you want to darken or warm your hair colour, go for lowlights which work in the same way but with darker sections of hair.

Wash in/Wash out – Colours that you wash in like a shampoo and lasts between one and twelve shampoos. These colourants

don't include any chemicals so they can darken your hair temporarily but not lighten.

Semi-permanent – These colours often include small amounts of hydrogen peroxide so they can slightly alter your hair colour but again, they cannot lighten. Semi-permanent colours last for up to 30 shampoos.

Permanent – Anything permanent will most likely include ammonia and hydrogen peroxide and can lighten or darken your hair colour. Before you apply, be certain the colour is exactly what you want because they don't ever wash out and you will have to grow the colour out. This can take years!

intensive care for hair

✱ If your hair is coloured or you use hairdryers, straightners or curlers often, your hair will need some serious TLC. You could get a conditioning treatment at the hairdressers when you go for your regular trim or you could give yourself the same treat at home.

✱ Rather than spending money on an expensive deep conditioner, you can make a great treatment from ordinary olive oil. Pour three tablespoons of oil for short hair, five for medium hair and seven for very long hair, into a bowl and warm up for sixty seconds in the microwave on a low setting.

✱ Now wash your hair as usual and gently massage the warm olive oil into the lengths of your hair. Once your hair is coated, wrap it in clingfilm – this might look silly but the heat from the plastic will help your hair absorb the oil. Wrap a warm towel around the clingfilm and relax for thirty minutes before washing the oil out thoroughly.

hair speak

❀ It's really good fun to look through hair magazines at new styles and talk to your hair stylist about the latest cuts and colouring techniques but it's easy to be confused by all the jargon. Here are a few common terms you might hear in the salon.

❀ Bangs – this is just another term for your fringe.

❀ Layers – if your hairdresser asks if you want layers, he's asking if you want your hair cut to graduated lengths, long at the bottom and shorter on the top. Layers makes your hair look thicker and are much more versatile than one length hair.

❀ Perm – This is short for 'permanent wave' and you really don't want one. Perms change your hair's natural texture and create curls but also dry out your hair and make it incredibly frizzy. If you really want curly hair make friends with heated rollers, don't turn to chemicals.

❀ Baliage – This is a form of highlighting where the colourist paints the bleach onto your hair with a brush.

4 a new you

A New You isn't really a completely true title. Make-up can change how you look but it can't change who you are – and more importantly, you shouldn't want it to! However, a new make-up look can give you bags of confidence and help bring out the **real** you.

There are lots of different looks in this section, perfect for every occasion. Take your inspiration from these pages and then play around with the look to individualise it. Maybe your First Date look will be better with a soft coral lip colour rather than a rose pink – keep experimenting until you find the perfect look for you. For the different looks, we've just listed the key items you'll need to make it work and items that might not be in your everyday make-up kit.

Just like everything in life, you have to keep trying new things – even make-up can get boring if you get stuck in a rut. Why not try some of these looks with your sisters and friends, or even your mum and your aunts – makeovers are a great way to bring girls together!

all about eyes

✳ Your eyes are the most expressive part of your body and the easiest to emphasise so really go for it and have fun experimenting.

✳ Before you start applying eye make-up, prep the delicate skin with foundation so your eye colour has something to cling to. Your eyelids can get greasy easily so it

might be a good idea to invest in an eye base if you're going to wear eye colour often.

✳ Always remember the skin around your eyes is thinner and more delicate than anywhere else on your body. If your regular cleanser can't shift all your eye make-up easily, you need an oil-free eye makeup remover. Soak a cotton wool pad in the remover and press it gently against your eye for a couple of seconds. When

you sweep the pad away, your eye make-up, including mascara, should come away easily.

✳ Don't be afraid to play with different colours around your eyes. If in doubt, keep them sheer and light to keep the look modern and fresh.

all about eyes

✳ Mascara is the easiest way to make the most of your eyes. Correctly applied mascara makes your eyes look bigger, whiter and sparklier whilst giving you thick, gorgeous lashes. So whether you're wearing eye colour or not, mascara is the easiest way to look gorgeous.

✳ The way you apply your eyeliner and eyeshadow can really make the most of your eye shape. Try these tricks to make the most of your eyes:

✳ If you have small eyes, line the lower rims with white or light beige eyeliner to make them look bigger.

✳ If your eyes are close together, lining your upper and lower lids from the centre out to the edge with a dark liner or shadow will make them seem further apart. Wide-set eyes should line the inside half of their eyes to make them seem closer together.

✳ Deep-set eyes should apply light neutral colours over the whole lid with a medium toned colour in the crease to make them stand out more.

✳ To make your eyes look fresher, apply a small dot of sparkly powder directly above your pupil.

luscious lips

✳ Great lip colour is easy to achieve and fun to play around with but every look has to start with soft, smooth lips. Once a week, use a lip exfoliator or rub a soft toothbrush gently over your lips to remove any dead skin. Apply a slick of lip balm immediately – petroleum jelly works perfectly.

✳ Why not have a go at mixing up your own lip colours? Use a cotton bud to scoop out the remains of an old lipstick and scrape it into a lip palette or an old lip balm pot.

Do this with several old colours, and then use your lip brush to mix two or three shades together. Your own, personal lipstick!

✻ There are a couple of colour rules with lipstick – If you've got pink toned skin, go for blue-toned colours. Anything too pink will make your skin look flushed while if you have a warmer skin tone, go for colours with orangey undertones,

✻ To work out your skin tone, try these easy tests:

Does your skin look better with gold or silver jewellery? Gold suits warm skin tones while silver flatters cool.

Can you see the veins on the inside of your wrists? People with warm skin tones will have veins that appear green whereas cool skin tones will have blue veins.

luscious lips

* Making the most of your lip shape is easy. You can still wear any colour, just choose your shade carefully and follow these rules:

* If your lips are thin stick to light colours for daytime to make them look larger. If you want to wear darker colours, avoid matte formulations, dot highlighter in the centre of your top and bottom lips and finish with a slick of gloss.

* Full lips can wear any lip colours but you're one of the lucky few that can get away with the palest beiges. For dramatic looks, play up your lips with bright reds and deep berry colours, keeping the rest of your face neutral.

* If your top lip is thinner and than your bottom lip, try and balance them out by lining the top lip with a neutral liner, just outside your natural lip line. Fill in both lips with a medium lip shade and sweep some gloss on to your top lip only.

blush baby

* Choosing the right blusher is as easy as looking in the mirror after you've been exercising and recreating that colour with make-up. It will most likely be a pink or peachy colour, as these tend to look the most natural. The darker your skin tone, the darker the shade of blush you can take.

* Blusher really brings your complexion to life. The right shade makes you look healthy and vibrant but the wrong shade will make you look ill and overly made up, so try out of different colours until you find the right one.

* For every day loveliness, the easiest way to wear blush is to brush the colour onto the apples of your cheeks. To make the most of your face shape, try out these tips:

* Square face – Soften your square face by dusting blush on the apples of your cheeks and blending upwards towards your temples

* Round face – To give your cheekbones more structure, sweep the blusher onto the centre of the cheeks and blend downwards, under your cheekbones.

✳ Heart-shaped face – Brush colour onto the lowest part of the apples of your cheeks. This will draw attention to the lower part of your face and balance out your wide cheeks.

✳ Long face – Sweep your blusher onto the apples of your cheeks and blend it back towards your ears to make you face look wider.

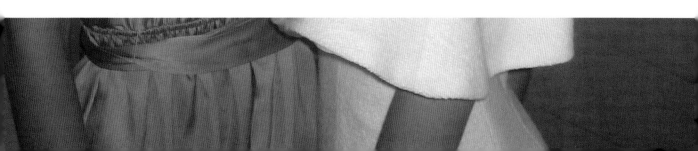

how to highlight

✳ Highlighters are far subtler than glitter make-up and draw attention to your best features without shouting about it. They're super easy to apply and make you look fresh and dewy even if you're wearing full foundation and powder.

✳ The sparkly pigments in today's highlighters reflect and break up light, making your skin glow and look more even. Young skins can take more sparkly make-up than older skins, as it tends to highlight any lines and imperfections as well.

✳ If you have pretty shoulders or want to show off a healthy tan, dot highlighter on your collarbones and blend. To make the most of high cheekbones, dot highlighter along the top of your cheekbones and blend outwards towards your temples. Never overload your face with highlighter or it will look greasy. Cheekbones and brow bones are alright, but not all over your cheeks and forehead. It's another classic case of less is more.

cool for school

✳ Make-up for school is all about subtlety and making the most of your natural features.

You will need:
Tinted moisturiser or foundation diluted with regular moisturiser
Pressed powder
Concealer
A pinky blusher
Lip balm
Brown mascara

✳ Start by applying foundation to your t-zone and then dabbing on concealer where it's needed. Seal your base with pressed powder.

✳ Swirl your blusher brush in your cheek colour, a soft pink should suit everyone and look natural enough for school. Knock any excess off the brush by tapping it on the back of your hand and then sweep across the apples of your cheeks.

✳ Now, take your mascara wand and wipe away any access on a tissue. Comb through your lashes to give some natural definition. If the colour clumps, comb through with an eyelash comb or an old mascara wand that you've washed clean.

✳ Finish off your cool school look with a dab of tinted lip balm to keep everything fresh and light.

weekend chic

✳ This is a great look for hanging out with your friends or going shopping. You don't want anything too dramatic that will need constant retouching – you'll be having way too much fun with your buds to be worried about reapplying your lipstick!

You will need:
Silvery lilac eyeshadow
Royal blue eyeliner pencil
Brown mascara
Clear gloss

✳ If you want to wear base, apply a light foundation or tinted moisturiser to your t-zone, dot concealer where needed and set with a dusting of loose powder.

✳ You don't need eyeshadow brushes for this look, just smudge the colour across your eyelid with your middle finger. You want to cover the lid right up to the crease and don't worry about it look too perfect. You can use any light sparkly colour but lilac seems to work well on most people.

✳ To really draw attention to your eyes, draw a thin line of royal blue eyeliner pencil along your top lash line. Smudge lightly with a cotton bud to lose any hard lines and

finish with two coats of brown mascara.

✳ To complete this easy look, you just need a slick of clear gloss and a sweeping of your blusher across the apples of your cheeks. Remember to take your clear gloss and pressed powder with you for touch ups.

first date!

＊ Ok, now you're probably nervous enough about your date without having to worry about your make-up! Once you've decided what you want to wear (something you're comfortable in), keep your make-up easy. Plus, your date wants to see you, not your make-up.

You will need:
Dove grey eyeshadow
White sparkly eyeshadow
Grey eyeliner pencil
Black mascara
Highlighter
Rose pink lipstick

＊ Firstly, apply your foundation and then concealer to any areas that need it – you don't want to be worrying about dark circles or spots on your date. Set the base with loose powder and dust away any excess with your large powder brush.

＊ Brush the dove grey eyeshadow up to the crease of your upper eyelid and then brush the sparkly white eyeshadow under your eyebrows. Draw the grey eyeliner pencil along your lower lashes, then, with a small eyeshadow brush, gently run the grey eyeshadow over the top to soften the line.

Smudge the grey eyeliner pencil along your upper lashes but only from the centre of your eyelid to the outside edge, extending it slightly into a small flick. This might take some practise so don't try it for the first time on the night of your date. Finish your eyes with two coats of black mascara to frame your eyes.

Your lips should look natural and pretty, so apply your rose pink lipstick straight from the tube, blotting twice. To really set off the look, dot a tiny amount of highlighter along your cheekbones, above your eyebrows and just above the cupid's bow of your top lip. Blend carefully until your skin is radiant and glowing.

party time!

✳ Time to party and time to try out some fun looks! You don't want to be running to the bathroom all night to check your make-up so here's a couple of fun ideas to accessorise your basic look.

✳ Try coloured mascara with contrasting eyeshadow to bring your eyes to life. Lemon shadow with royal blue mascara, lime green eyeshadow with aubergine mascara, pale pink eye shadow with dark green mascara – try out the different combos until you find one you like.

✳ Keep the rest of your face really simple and then load your eyelids with glitter and mascara. Use a glitter spray to add some sparkle to your hair.

✳ Apply a berry lipstick with your finger, smudging it well into your lips. Blot the colour and reapply until there is no finish left, just a deep stain of colour.

✳ Or keep your make-up simple and use hair mascara to colour the tips of your hair – try hot pink or electric blue.

fun and funky

✳ This is a great look for going out, but you might want to practise a few times at home first. Eyeliner is the trickiest thing to learn how to apply and the vivid colour of this look might take some getting used to!

You will need:
Turquoise or purple liquid eyeliner
Black mascara
Clear lip balm or petroleum jelly

✳ Your base should be perfect for this look as you're going to be drawing a lot of attention to your

face! Apply your base with a sponge, conceal any blemishes and dark circles, then load a velvet puff with loose powder and press against your skin. Brush away any excess with your large powder brush.

✻ Prep your eyes with foundation to even out the skin tone and give your eyeliner something to cling to. Rest your elbow on a steady surface and draw your eyeliner across your eyelid in one smooth motion, flicking half a centimetre outwards from the outer corner.

The line should be fairly thick and completely even.

✻ Repeat on your lower lid, joining the two lines up on the outside lid with a small flick. Always flick upwards, a downward flick pulls your entire face down. Leave the rest of your eyelid bare for impact.

✻ Finish off with one coat of mascara and a matte, but soft mouth – clear lip balm is perfect.

pretty pastels

* Pastel colours really brighten your face and make you look fresh and pretty. You can use just about any pastel colour from petal pink to baby blue.

You will need:
Pastel eye shadow – a light and medium shade
Black mascara
Pink or peach lip gloss

* Your base should be fresh and light for this look. Concealer and loose powder should be enough to even out your skin tone.

✳ Using a small eyeshadow brush, dust the medium shade onto the inner corners of your upper eyelids and blend out to the centre of the lid. Next dust the lighter shade from the centre of your eyelid, out to the outer corner of your lid. Blend the two colours together and up, just above the crease.

✳ Dust the same lighter shade onto the lower lid, blending into the lower lash line. Contrast the light fresh look with a coat of black mascara on the upper and lower lashes.

✳ Finish your look with a slick of pretty lip gloss and a swirl of pastel blush on the apples of your cheeks.

metallic mayhem

＊ Metallics create dramatic make-up looks that suit everyone. If you're pale, go for silver while warmer skin tones can take gold or bronze make-up.

You will need:
Gold or silver liquid liner
Gold, silver or bronze powder shadow
Pale iridescent cream shadow
Black mascara

＊ Start with a carefully applied base with foundation, concealer and loose powder. Your skin should be soft and velvety to offset the harsh metallics. Keep blusher very soft and dusted on the top of your cheekbones.

＊ Begin your eyes by applying the iridescent cream all over the

eyelid to create a glowy base. With a rounded eyeshadow brush, sweep the powder shadow on your upper lid up to the crease, creating a solid block of colour.

* Apply the liner in one clean sweep, keeping the line close to your lashes and extending in a small flick. Don't line your lower lashes, just brush a thin line of shadow close to the lashes. Curl your lashes and finish with two coats of black mascara to frame your eyes.

take it as red

✳ Red lipstick is a great look, clean, fun and sophisticated. If you're nervous or think it's too old for you then just hold off until you're ready, there's no rush. You could also try a sheer red gloss or lip balm until you're comfortable with the colour.

You will need:
A red lip liner
A satiny red lipstick
A lip brush
Tissues

✳ If you're ready to go for it, there's a shade of red right for everyone.

✳ Keep the rest of your face neutral to keep the emphasis on your lips, a neat base, soft blush on the apples of your cheeks and brown/black mascara on your lashes. If you think your face needs balancing, try a thin line of grey liner smudged into your upper lash line.

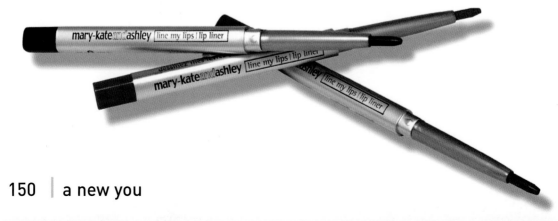

✻ Before you apply the lip colour, your lips should be soft and clean – exfoliate, moisturise with a lip balm and then prep with foundation. Next, take a red lip pencil and lightly outline your natural lip line.

✻ Most lipsticks look best applied from the tube or smudged with your finger, but a neat red mouth really does look best when applied with a lip brush. Fill in your pencil outline then blot with tissue and fill again.

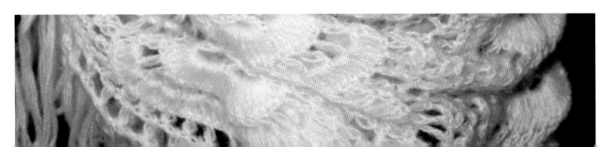

smoke and mirrors

* Smokey eyes are fun, fresh and modern. Traditionally, smokey looks were made using black or grey eyeshadow but you can get just as cool a look from soft brown, blue or even green. This is a glam look and not for every day so save it for parties.

You will need:
A kohl or eyeliner pencil
A dark and light shade of one colour charcoal, mossy green or royal blue are great
Black mascara
Cotton buds

* It's best to keep the rest of your face simple, a cream blush and lip balm or clear gloss will balance out the strength of your eyes.

* Start by drawing a line all the way across the top of your lashes with your kohl pencil or eyeliner. Brush the darkest shade of your shadow on top of the liner and then smudge with a cotton bud. Use a round shadow brush to brush the lighter shade of your shadow up to the crease of your eyelid and blend to avoid hard lines.

* Next, repeat on your bottom lid, leaving out the kohl pencil or eyeliner if you want a softer look. Smudge again with a cotton bud and finish with a coat of mascara.

Hopefully, now that you've finished the book, you have got all the basic beauty know-how to create your own signature look. Will it be dark eyes or red lips? Sheer pastels or electric blue eyeliner?

The important things to remember are to take good care of your skin – inside and out – always wash your face when you've been wearing make-up and if in doubt, stick to colours that suit your skin tone.

The great thing about experimenting with make-up is that you can always wash it off; it's only make-up after all. If you don't like the green eye shadow that looked so cool on your best friend, wipe it away and try the hot pink. It's that easy.

Make-up shouldn't make your life more complicated, it should only make it more fun. Now you know all the beauty secrets! Get the girls around and start having fun!

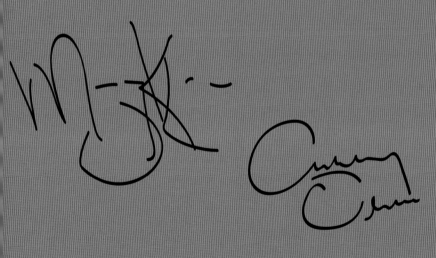

From Los Angeles to New York, the latest fragrance creations from

the mary-kateandashley brand

L.A. Style and *N.Y. Chic*

150 ml Body Mist at £4.99 and Edt 50 ml at £9.99
Available now at Boots, Superdrug, Asda and select beauty retailers

For further information, please call Selective Beauty at: +44 (0)20 7620 2333

www.mary-kateandashley.com

TM & © 2006 Dualstar Entertainment Group, LLC.

DUALSTAR
ENTERTAINMENT
GROUP

Selective Beauty

mary-kateandashley™
COSMETICS

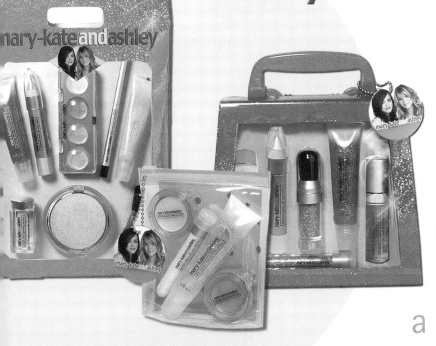

hypnotise
with dazzling eyes

add a hint of shimmer

seal it with
a kiss of glimmer

gift sets available at *Boots*

www.mary-kateandashley.com